Parent Council® Selection

"Contains valuable shortcuts and hints to help you
enhance your teaching, manage you and enjoy
greater success on the
    —*Learning*

**Over 300
strategies, tips, and helpful hints
for teachers of all grades**

by **Craig Mitchell**

with **Pamela Espeland**

free spirit ⟨ Works
for kids®
PUBLiSHiNG®

371.102
MiT

12/08 DONATION

Library of Congress Cataloging-in-Publication Data
Mitchell, Craig, 1962–
    Teach to reach : over 300 strategies, tips, and helpful hints for teachers of all
grades / Craig Mitchell with Pamela Espeland.
    p.   cm.
    ISBN 1-57542-010-4
    1. Teaching–Miscellanea. 2. Classroom management–Miscellanea.
I. Espeland, Pamela   .   II. Title.
LB1027.M5414   1996   96-7812
371.1'02–dc20   CIP

Cover and book design by MacLean & Tuminelly

15 14 13 12 11 10 9
Printed in Canada

Free Spirit Publishing Inc.
217 Fifth Avenue North, Suite 200
Minneapolis, MN 55401-1299
(612) 338-2068
help4kids@freespirit.com
www.freespirit.com

DEDICATION

To the many students and teachers I have worked with over the years. They have taught me valuable lessons both in and out of the classroom.

C.M.

To John, my husband, and Jonah, my son — two of the best teachers I've ever had.

P.L.E.

ACKNOWLEDGMENTS

I am grateful to Dr. Felice Kaufmann for her support and words of inspiration.

I owe my brother, Wayne Mitchell, many paid fishing trips for the time he spent examining each and every word of my manuscript.

Finally, I would like to thank my wife, Melanie, who is always there to remind me of why I became a teacher. She has been an invaluable sounding board and my best friend.

C.M.

INTRODUCTION

Teach to Reach is a practical resource for all teachers who are looking for ways to enhance their teaching skills, their classroom environment, their school, and their students' success at learning. The ideas in this book are meant to help first-year teachers, those with many years of experience, student teachers, and substitute teachers — anyone who faces a roomful of students for a day, a week, a year, or a lifetime.

As teachers, we are also students. We should never stop seeking, learning, and practicing new ways to develop and present lesson materials, communicate with our students, and make our classrooms positive places to be. Teaching is a process of helping others to learn and grow, but it should also be a process of constant self-improvement.

In teaching, as in any other profession, there are "tricks of the trade." A comment I often hear in staff rooms and at conferences is, "We should get together and share our ideas." Of course we should, but we seldom do. We get so involved in our daily responsibilities that we don't take time to pool our knowledge. In my own years of teaching, I have been fortunate to work with many fine teachers who were willing to open their classrooms to me. I have learned a great deal from them — about being a better teacher, focusing my skills, and enjoying my profession even more. This book comes out of my own experience, but it owes a great debt to my colleagues who generously shared their "tricks" with me.

The strategies, tips, and hints in this book are not subject-specific. You won't find ways to help your students learn the multiplication tables or use proper punctuation. You will find hundreds of practical, encouraging, creative suggestions for making school more meaningful and fun for everyone, from students to staff. I have divided the book into sections, but it's my hope that you can turn to any page and find something useful — food for thought, an idea to try, a word or phrase that will pique your curiosity or lift your spirits. You may disagree with some of my ideas, which probably means that you have already developed effective strategies of your own. What's important to remember is that there is no single "perfect" or "right" way to teach. We all need to keep our eyes and ears open; we all need to be willing to change and grow; we all need to cooperate, collaborate, and share what we know. Only then can we truly promote and celebrate learning.

I'd love to hear how *Teach to Reach* works for you. And I'd love to learn about your teaching strategies, if you care to share them with me. Please write to me c/o Free Spirit Publishing, 217 Fifth Avenue North, Suite 200, Minneapolis, MN 55401-1299.

I wish you the very best in your teaching career.

Craig Mitchell

Teach to reach your students;
teach them to reach
for the knowledge and wisdom
you have to offer.

Starting the New School Year

During the summer, most of us don't spend all day, every day talking, so it's not uncommon to experience hoarseness and sore throats during the first month of school. Get your voice in shape by singing your favorite songs out loud. Start 2–3 weeks before school begins, and increase the number of songs you sing as the first day of school approaches.

Remember that teaching can be a physically taxing job. Especially if you spend much of each day on your feet, you'll want to build endurance and improve flexibility in the weeks before school begins. Take brisk walks, go for bike rides, do stretching exercises, or whatever you prefer.

A week or two before school starts, write personal notes to all of the students on your class list. Introduce yourself, say that you look forward to seeing them, and give a hint about something fun and interesting they'll be learning soon.

On the first day of school, stand at the entrance to your classroom and greet your students as they arrive. Smile at everyone and welcome those you know by name.

Be very organized on the first day of school. Set the tone for the whole year by showing that you use class time efficiently. List the day's activities on the board and have all materials and worksheets ready to hand out. Tell students what to do with their jackets, bags, supplies, and food.

Include some hands-on activities during the first day of school, as most students will be eager to begin.

Teach page set-up on the first day of school. Tell your students that all of the work they do in class — papers, assignments, notebook pages, handouts, tests, etc. — must include their name, the date, and a title (*examples:* "Math Homework for Page 23," "Spelling Words," "Hopes and Dreams Essay," "Research Report on Tadpoles"). Create an example on poster board and display it in the classroom.

Teach your students how to use an assignment notebook. Check notebooks daily or weekly for the first month or until you're confident that your students are making the most of this valuable tool.

Review your student supplies list before sending it home to parents. Is it up-to-date? Is anything missing? Can some items be dropped from the list? Talk to parents and other staff members about your list, and solicit their comments and suggestions. Keep in mind those families who might not be able to afford school supplies, and those who have many children to equip.

Contact local discount stores that carry office and school supplies. Ask if they're willing to post your supplies list or keep copies on hand for parents; if they are, you'll point parents in their direction. If your school or district has many students, ask about discounts or money-saving coupons for parents.

Consider having your students use folders instead of three-ring binders. They are less bulky and easier to carry back and forth between school and home.

Teach your students how to travel through the halls quietly, politely, and efficiently. Practice with them until you feel confident that they have learned proper hallway behavior – no jumping, hitting door frames, banging lockers, cutting corners, running, skipping, etc.

Rehearse and practice classroom routines until everyone understands them. Instead of assuming that students automatically know what to do, make your expectations clear. Once routines have been established, monitor closely and retrain when necessary.

Talk openly and honestly with your students about cheating. If your school has an official policy on cheating, share it with them and post it in your classroom.

Discourage whining in your classroom. Students who regularly complain or grumble ("Do we *have* to?" "We just *had* a quiz!" "This is *boring!*") can demoralize an entire group. Tell your students that if they have real problems or legitimate concerns, they should bring them to you in person. Or they might use the "Let's Talk" box (see page 22).

Just because your students "should have learned" a particular skill or concept before arriving in your classroom doesn't mean they *have* learned it. Be alert to what's missing and get help from support staff when needed.

Be prepared to teach study skills. No matter what grade you teach, you may find that some students don't know how to study, while others need a refresher course in basic study skills.

Make a list of 10–20 things you want to accomplish by the end of the school year. Keep your list in your daily calendar or notebook, check it often, and note your progress.

Have your students make lists of things they want to accomplish by the end of the year.

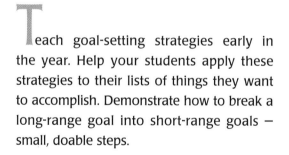

Teach goal-setting strategies early in the year. Help your students apply these strategies to their lists of things they want to accomplish. Demonstrate how to break a long-range goal into short-range goals — small, doable steps.

Create a cooperative classroom climate from the moment your students first enter your room. Make everyone feel welcome; build teamwork with activities that encourage cooperation and have a high chance of success.

On the Friday of the first week of school, give your students something to look forward to on Monday.

Creating a Nurturing Classroom

Always be at the entrance to your classroom and greet your students by name as they arrive. Some teachers welcome their students with positive comments and a handshake.

Remember that *all* of your students need to be heard, acknowledged, appreciated, respected, accepted, and taken seriously. They *all* need your support, understanding, and approval.

Avoid labeling students ("the smart one," "the funny one," "the quiet one"). Every student has a name. Use your students' names when you talk *to* them, when you talk *about* them, and even when you *think* about them.

Talk with your students about how people are different (looks, abilities, race, economic background, gender, etc.) but also very much alike (basic needs, feelings, hopes, etc.). Emphasize that *all* human beings deserve the chance to learn, grow, and achieve.

Many parents and students are rightfully concerned about sex-role stereotyping and gender equity. Make it clear that in your classroom, everyone is educationally equal. *Examples:* Steer away from "girls vs. boys" activities. Expect all students to follow the same rules. Unless you teach at an all-male school, take care not to use phrases like "You guys are doing great!" Be sure to call on girls as often as boys.

Learn about your students' diverse ethnic and cultural backgrounds. Make learning activities multicultural. Invite students, parents, and guests to visit your classroom and talk about their cultures and traditions. Education leads to tolerance, acceptance, understanding – and friendship.

Why should students have to ask permission to go to the restroom? It's humiliating! Keep a laminated hall pass by the door and tell students that they can use it whenever they need it – as long as they leave quietly, return promptly, and behave appropriately in the halls and in the restroom.

Communicate one-on-one with each of your students at least once a day, either verbally or in writing. This shows that you are aware of them and care about them as individuals.

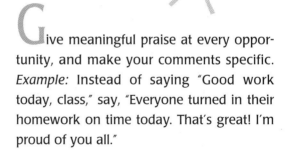

Give meaningful praise at every opportunity, and make your comments specific. *Example:* Instead of saying "Good work today, class," say, "Everyone turned in their homework on time today. That's great! I'm proud of you all."

Have a confidential "Let's Talk" box in your classroom. Explain that students can use the "Let's Talk" box to communicate with you, that you are the *only* person who will open the box, and that you will check it for messages at the end of each day. Students might use the "Let's Talk" box to comment on classroom issues, personal problems, happy occasions, academic difficulties, exciting events, or whatever else they choose. They don't have to sign their names unless they want a personal reply from you. Students might also use the "Let's Talk" box to request a meeting with you, stating briefly the reason for the meeting and a time that works for them. Respond to signed notes as soon as possible.

Instruct your students to listen respectfully while someone else is talking, even if they don't agree with what the speaker is saying. Emphasize that interruptions, criticism, and ridicule are not allowed. Model this behavior by example.

Ask your students privately for permission to model or display their work before holding it up or putting it on the bulletin board. Respect their wishes.

When your students work especially hard or cooperate especially well, write a big note of thanks and congratulations on the board. When you can, write individual personal notes on special stationery.

Teach your students the basics of stress reduction and stress management. Take a course, read a book, and share what you learn.

If you wake up in a bad mood, do whatever you can to cheer yourself up before you arrive at school. Nobody needs a crabby teacher.

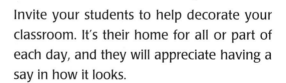

Change your seating plan and room set-up throughout the school year. There are many ways you can group students and their desks or tables. Ask for students' input — where would they like to sit? Does anyone have ideas for a new seating plan? Strike a balance between moving too often (distracting) and not often enough (dull).

Invite your students to help decorate your classroom. It's their home for all or part of each day, and they will appreciate having a say in how it looks.

As you post notices, announcements, student work, art, posters, maps, etc., around your classroom, put yourself in your students' shoes. Are the materials at their eye level? Is the print big enough for them to read? Are sign-up sheets within easy reach?

Communicate your delight in learning and teaching — in your attitude, general demeanor, facial expressions, body language, and tone of voice.

Except for the necessary educational modifications, treat your mentally and physically challenged students like everyone else. Talk to them, joke with them, praise them, correct their mistakes, answer their questions, and follow through on consequences for inappropriate behavior.

Be sensitive to the needs of your left-handed students. *Examples:* Right-handed scissors can be uncomfortable for them, and three-ring binders can interfere with hand movement when writing. Don't seat left-handed students immediately to the right of right-handed students. Remedy other problem situations or (better yet) prevent them before they occur.

Set up a student council in your classroom so students can express their needs and wishes on an ongoing basis. Structure and monitor the program to ensure that all students are represented. Thank and reward those students who volunteer their time, and plan special events for them throughout the year.

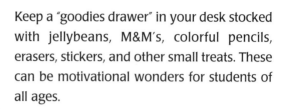

Keep a "goodies drawer" in your desk stocked with jellybeans, M&M's, colorful pencils, erasers, stickers, and other small treats. These can be motivational wonders for students of all ages.

Don't make promises to your students unless you're sure you can keep them. Expect them to honor their promises to you.

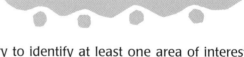

Try to identify at least one area of interest for each of your students. (Some students will have multiple interests; for others, you'll have to dig for this information.) Occasionally give assignments that relate to their interests. This makes learning more meaningful and fun.

Encourage your students to pursue their passions and interests both in and out of school. Invite them to tell you about their hobbies and collections. Share your passions and interests with them, and celebrate those you have in common.

Everyone has the potential to become an expert at something. Encourage your students to develop their areas of expertise and share them with the class in special reports or projects.

Make time every day to talk with individual students. Select 2–3 students each day and speak to each one for 3–4 minutes. You might use this "quality time" to discuss school or home situations that are affecting the student's learning; physical, social, emotional, and academic needs; interests, hobbies, or passions; or anything else the student wants to talk about.

Hold weekly class meetings. Ask for volunteers to plan the agenda, record the minutes, chair the meeting, and time the agenda items. Rotate responsibilities. Class meetings are an excellent way to deal with class problems, plan interesting activities, and give students practice in discussing issues and organizing events.

Have high expectations for *all* of your students, not just those you perceive as the brightest and most capable. When you make it clear that you expect *all* students to succeed in your classroom, they will!

Teach your students how to give and receive compliments. Show them the way and offer plenty of opportunities for practice.

Teach your students to use "I-statements" instead of accusations. *Example:* "I don't like it when Terry calls me names," not "Terry always calls me names!"

Teach your students to ask for what they need instead of making demands. *Example:* "I need Terry to stop calling me names," not "Terry better stop calling me names or else!"

Tell your students that "can't" is a four-letter word you'd rather not hear. Encourage them to overcome their doubts and fears. Acknowledge their successes and remind them that you're always there to help.

Be alert to behavior changes and signs of emotional distress in your students. If you're concerned about a particular student, arrange to talk privately with him or her. Express your concern and emphasize that you care. Don't hesitate to seek advice from your school counselor or psychologist.

Remember that there are two sides to every character trait. Focus on the positive. *Examples:* Is a student nosy . . . or curious? Bossy . . . or a good leader? Picky . . . or meticulous? Weird . . . or unique? Noisy . . . or enthusiastic? Sullen . . . or reserved? You can *choose* how to perceive your students.

When a student is especially difficult, challenging, and frustrating, make a list of five positive things about him or her. Focus on those.

Never criticize an individual student's work or behavior in front of the class. Especially when we're angry, it's tempting to target a particular student and "make an example" of him or her. There are always more positive and effective ways to deal with problems.

Be careful about praising individual students in front of the class. Many of us will say something like, "I notice Alex is doing a good job of sitting quietly today." But the student might feel uncomfortable about being singled out, and others in the classroom might resent it — and take out their resentment on the student when you're not around.

Never penalize the whole class for the actions of one or a few. Instead, take a "positive peer pressure" approach and reward the whole class for helping problem students fit in and succeed. *Example:* If one student often talks out of turn, those sitting around him can quietly remind him to raise his hand. At the end of the day (or the end of a lesson), praise the whole class for remembering to raise their hands.

Whenever you're about to lose patience with a student, stop and think about how it feels to be on the receiving end of a teacher's disapproval.

Communicate in words and actions that you care about your students and you're there to help them every day. Remind them often and make yourself available. *Example:* Post a sign-up sheet for students who want to meet with you privately before school, after school, or (in special cases) during your prep time or break. Encourage students to use the "Let's Talk" box (see page 22) to request meetings with you.

Be observant. Notice and offer positive comments on new haircuts, new shoes, ear-to-ear smiles, improved and/or positive attitudes, helpful behaviors, and so on.

Encourage your students to laugh and smile. Create a "humor corner" in your classroom where they can post their favorite jokes and cartoons. Keep a supply of joke books, cartoons, and funny audiocassettes on hand, and lighten up lessons with brief "joke breaks."

Use your sense of humor with students, staff, and parents. Share appropriate jokes and funny comments. We all need a good laugh from time to time, and smiling faces create a more positive and productive learning environment.

Laugh and joke with your colleagues in front of your students. This shows that teachers are "regular people" and school is a friendly place.

Practice random acts of kindness in your classroom, school, home, and community, and encourage your students to do the same. Have a "Random Acts" box where students can drop in brief descriptions of their own random acts — unsigned. Start each week by reading examples pulled from the "Random Acts" box. At the end of the year, compile a "Random Acts" book for your students to bring home. Or make the book a class project.

Keep class rules and routines short and simple. The less complicated they are, the more likely your students will follow them.

Let your students make their own class rules. Invite them to brainstorm suggestions; have them vote on the 5–10 "top rules"; ask volunteers to make a poster of the rules to display in the classroom.

A few weeks after posting the class rules, review them with your students. Are the rules reasonable? Invite suggestions and improvements.

Set aside 5–10 minutes each day for "sharing time." While the rest of the class sits comfortably, individual students take turns sharing their thoughts about school, home, hobbies, friends, community events, world events, or whatever else they want to talk about. The only rules are: 1) students volunteer to share – they aren't assigned or expected to share; 2) only one speaker at a time; and 3) no criticism or ridicule allowed. Some classes have a "Share Chair" where students sit to speak and answer questions. Be sure to preview all items and topics in advance.

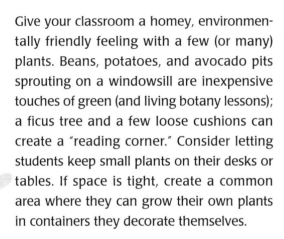

Give your classroom a homey, environmentally friendly feeling with a few (or many) plants. Beans, potatoes, and avocado pits sprouting on a windowsill are inexpensive touches of green (and living botany lessons); a ficus tree and a few loose cushions can create a "reading corner." Consider letting students keep small plants on their desks or tables. If space is tight, create a common area where they can grow their own plants in containers they decorate themselves.

Are pets allowed in your school? A rabbit, a gerbil, a gecko, goldfish — any and all can add life to your classroom (and

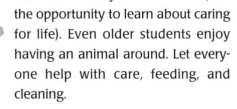

the opportunity to learn about caring for life). Even older students enjoy having an animal around. Let everyone help with care, feeding, and cleaning.

Promote curiosity in your classroom. If a student asks a question you can't answer, 1) promise to find the answer and get back to the student as soon as you can, 2) point the student toward a resource you know contains the answer, or 3) work together to find the answer. Of course, there may be questions that don't have answers. These are great opportunities for thoughtful discussion.

If you don't know the answer
to a question, don't fake it.

If you don't know the answer to
a question, maybe one of your
students does. Ask.

If you give an answer that you later
find out was wrong, admit it.

Display your country's flag in your classroom; encourage patriotism and respect. Talk to your students about what the flag represents and the history behind it. If some students aren't allowed to participate in these activities for religious reasons, give them other options for "flag time."

Make music part of your classroom environment. Soft, soothing instrumental music is a wonderful backdrop for story writing, poetry, song writing, movement education, art, and many other subjects and activities. Try bright classical music, world music, or light jazz as a middle-of-the-day energizer.

Create a class song. Establish guidelines for the lyrics (*examples:* keep them positive and uplifting; emphasize teamwork, learning, goals, and school spirit) and hold a contest. Students can create original music or write lyrics to fit a popular melody. Post the song in your classroom and practice it often.

Thank students individually for any gifts and cards they bring you throughout the year. If you plan to display or use items you receive from your students, make sure that *all* gifts get their moment in the spotlight.

Treasure any gift a student gives
you, no matter how small.

If you're watching a video, reading
a story, or having a class discussion
that touches you deeply, don't be
afraid to let your feelings show.

Getting
and Staying
Organized

Be punctual. When you show up late for class in the morning or after breaks, you set a poor example. Problems can arise between the time the bell rings and you enter the classroom. Plus every minute you're late represents lost teaching and learning time.

Keep your desk neatly organized inside and out. You'll find things more easily, file things more efficiently, and be a good role model.

Invite students to share their personal organizing tips (different colored folders for different subjects? a notebook for keeping track of homework assignments? colored pens or pencils for taking notes?). Collect their ideas and post them in the classroom.

Tidy up your classroom on a daily basis. Make students responsible for various tasks and post a duty board. Students should straighten up their own desks and work surfaces each day before leaving.

Delegate various jobs in the classroom. Even younger students are capable of planning class celebrations, organizing and completing tasks, introducing people in assemblies, and arranging bulletin boards. Your workload will decrease and your students will become more involved with their own learning.

If you must leave your students alone in your room even for a moment, lock any sensitive materials in your desk, and be sure to take your keys.

At the end of each day, briefly summarize the day's activities and highlights. You might list them on the board and read them aloud. This gives your students something to say besides "Fine" or "Nothing" when their parents ask "How was school?" or "What did you do in school today?"

Keep notices, handouts, and permission slips on a table or desk near the exit door so you don't forget them in the end-of-the-day rush. Assign one or more students to pass them out as the others leave.

51

Develop an after-school routine for completing tasks. Prioritize paper-marking, lesson-planning, meetings, classroom organization tasks, etc., then get busy! The sooner you establish an effective system, the less time you'll waste and the more efficient you'll be.

Survey your classroom and answer these questions honestly: Are you a pack rat? Are you actually *using* all of the teaching materials you have collected? Cut down on the clutter in your classroom. If there are materials you're not using, take them home or donate them to other teachers.

Plan to do your photocopying during your prep block or after school. In most schools, the photocopy machine is in heavy demand before classes begin in the morning. Avoid the stress and confusion.

Keep a notebook listing any books and supplies you loan to other staff members. Document who borrowed what, when you expect it back, and when it is returned.

Write your name and telephone number on the cover and one inside page of every book you own and keep at school. This will make it easier to retrieve books whose covers are torn off or lost.

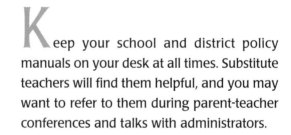

Keep your school and district policy manuals on your desk at all times. Substitute teachers will find them helpful, and you may want to refer to them during parent-teacher conferences and talks with administrators.

Hang a large yearly calendar in the staff room and highlight upcoming school events. This helps to avoid double-booking, facilitates planning, and informs the custodial crew of functions that affect their job duties. Some schools buy erasable calendars and pens to accommodate changes.

End all staff meetings with a brief summary of the meeting, thank-yous, and a schedule of upcoming meeting dates. Distribute meeting minutes to everyone involved to avoid confusion and misunderstandings in the future.

Take a look around your room. Is there an area that's always messy (probably meaning that it's overused) or always neat (underused)? Are the examples of student work on display several weeks or months old? Is it time to replace the posters on the walls? Could the desks use re-arranging? Where in the room do students tend to congregate, and why? Stand in the hall for a few moments, then walk into your room as if you're seeing it for the first time. What else needs improving, freshening, changing?

Come up with a plan for times when you are called out of the classroom for an emergency. Do your students know what to do and how to proceed with their work in your absence? Role play and rehearse various situations.

Whenever you must leave your room for any amount of time, let your neighboring teachers know.

Use clear plastic menu holders (you've seen them in restaurants) to display assignments, daily agendas, lesson outlines, etc. You can usually find these vertical stands in office supply stores.

Develop organized procedures for those classroom activities that are messy and time-consuming. When using paints, tools, or other materials, give clear instructions before beginning the hands-on part of the lesson. Establish a clean-up plan, delegate responsibilities, and assign student monitors.

Teach your students to be responsible for their own supplies. *Example:* Students who forget or misplace an item needed for a particular lesson may borrow from your "supply bank," but they must give you something as "collateral" to be returned when they give the borrowed item back to you. Keep a current and accurate list of items borrowed and returned. Tell your students that borrowing from the "bank" more than three times during a given week will result in a phone call to their parents, followed by a note about the supplies that are missing or needed.

Always have something to write with and on. You never know when inspiration might strike, or when you might hear or read an interesting idea, come across a book title you'll want to follow up on, or meet someone whose name you'll want to remember. Carry a pen or pencil and a small note-book, pack of 3"x 5" cards, pad of Post-It notes, or pocket calendar.

If you take daily attendance on a computer, back up the information in your notebook. Computers can crash; diskettes can get lost or misplaced. Be safe!

If you do most of your record-keeping, writing, and lesson planning on a computer, back up your files daily. Encourage your students to make copies of their work, and store the diskettes in a safe place (in the school office, at home, locked in your desk). It only takes one computer crash or lost diskette to reinforce the need for redundancy.

Keep a daily teaching journal. Each day after your students leave, grab a refreshment and reflect. Write a 5-minute journal entry about the day, with brief notes about teaching strategies that went well (and those that didn't), student successes (and difficulties), student responses to a new unit or activity, student relationships, etc. This practice will be very therapeutic, plus it will give you a "reference book" filled with potential report-card comments. Date all entries.

Routinely check your mail slot or message box throughout the day (during breaks works best for most teachers). It's easy to miss important notices and deadlines if you don't make this a habit.

Keep your filing up-to-date and organized. Each day, spend 5–10 minutes going through incoming mail, newsletters, catalogs, magazines, etc. Assign each piece to 1) the recycling bin, 2) the trash (if not recyclable), 3) a clearly marked folder in a file cabinet for future reference, or 4) an action file on your desk. Mark or stamp each piece you keep with the date received.

Invest in a self-inking day-date "RECEIVED" stamp. Use it to stamp mail, notes from parents, student papers, correspondence, memos, etc., as soon as you get them.

If you find yourself shuffling a piece of paper or mail more than once, it's time to act on it. Use it, file it, follow up on it, or toss it.

Delivering a Successful Lesson

When you're teaching a new subject or skill, give students a chance to prove what they have learned at various points along the way. Keep teaching those who haven't yet mastered the material; allow those who have achieved mastery to work on enrichment or hands-on activities that are related to the subject, or to pursue learning projects of their own. In other words, don't hold more capable students back while the others catch up.

Whenever you begin a new lesson or unit, relate it to something your students have already learned. This puts the new material in a familiar context and gives students confidence in their ability to learn it.

Face your students when you talk to them. Words can get garbled against the chalkboard.

Ask open-ended questions to stimulate discussion. Questions that require simple yes-or-no answers don't lead to learning. *Example:* Ask "How did the boy escape from the cave?" not "Did the boy escape from the cave?" Other good open-ended question starters are "Who?" "What?" "Why?" "When?" "Where?" and "In what way?"

Legible handwriting may be a dying art, but not in your classroom! Print and write neatly on worksheets, overheads, charts, and the chalkboard.

Avoid repeating instructions several times. Get your students' attention before explaining what you want them to do; ask individuals or groups to repeat your instructions to the class. Write or draw detailed instructions on the board so students can refer to them if they forget a step or two.

When teaching art lessons, have samples available that show the project in various stages from beginning to end. In most cases, this makes lengthy explanations unnecessary.

Make your teaching cues simple yet interesting. Use sounds, silly phrases, hand movements, symbols, musical interludes, and other creative devices to get your students' attention and indicate when you are moving from one subject or task to another. Ask your students to suggest cues for you to use.

Have students spend 2–3 minutes after a lesson silently reflecting on what they have learned or experienced. Invite volunteers to share their reflections. Or you might ask students to write down their thoughts and pass them along to you – a good way to get feedback on your teaching.

Don't dismiss your students for room changes, lunch breaks, or recess until you're ready to let them go. Have you properly closed your lesson? Have you clearly explained any homework assignments? Have you answered questions? Explain that the sound of the bell isn't the signal to get up and leave. They should wait for you to dismiss them. This ensures that the instruction part of the class is completed, plus it's more respectful.

Preview all videos and television programs before showing them to your students. It's worth your time to avoid potential embarrassment, battles with parents, and problems with administrators.

Bring your own talents and interests into the classroom. Chess, inventions, carpentry, cooking, gardening, song writing, etc., can all find their way into lessons.

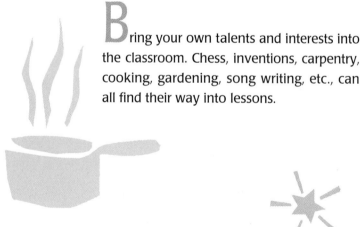

Plan and prepare each day's lessons at least a day in advance. This will prevent panic and problems if you become ill or are called away for meetings and phone calls before classes begin. Some teachers keep a file folder on their desk that includes the next 1–2 days of lesson plans and all required materials, in case of unexpected absences. You might label this folder "Attention: Substitute Teacher!"

Whenever possible, go beyond the textbook to make lessons exciting and immediate. *Example:* If you're studying water life, invite a scuba diver to visit your classroom, complete with diving equipment and slides. Plan a field trip to a nearby pond, lake, river, stream, or ocean. Ask park rangers and naturalists to speak to your class. Design hands-on projects for your students to do.

Invite and encourage questions. Tell your students that a lesson isn't finished until at least three provocative, in-depth questions have been asked.

Taking Care
of Yourself

Never forget that teaching is one of the world's most important jobs. And that makes you one of the world's most important people.

If you have work to do during your break, don't take it to the staff room. Stay in your (empty) classroom or find a quiet corner of the library.

Always allow a little more time for class projects, performances, introductions to new units, presentations, etc., than you think you'll need. You'll feel relaxed instead of pressured.

Remember that teaching is your job, not your whole life. Family, friends, faith, fun, and community are all important to maintaining your balance and sanity. We all know that teaching can become a 24-hours-a-day obsession if we let it.

Take the vacations you earn. Don't spend your vacation days at school; don't surround yourself with school books and materials. Enjoy your time off and try to experience a change of scenery. If it seems appropriate, share your vacation experiences with your students. Bring in postcards, slides, journal excerpts, photos, and/or souvenirs and let your students learn more about you and new places.

Pace yourself during hectic times of the school year. Teach lessons that require less planning, preparation, and paper marking; let students pursue independent projects and studies.

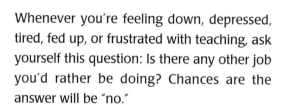

Whenever you're feeling down, depressed, tired, fed up, or frustrated with teaching, ask yourself this question: Is there any other job you'd rather be doing? Chances are the answer will be "no."

Keep teaching for as long as you feel committed and enthusiastic. If your interest lags, take courses, read journals and books, seek help from your peers, consider a change in your teaching assignment or school, attend a conference, or take a leave of absence.

Your desk is your domain. Students should not use it without your permission, and they definitely shouldn't turn it into a dumping ground for their papers, books, lunches, and jackets.

If your school must use portable classrooms, try not to stay in one for more than two years in a row. Ask to be moved so you aren't permanently isolated from the rest of the school population.

If you teach in a portable classroom, never leave your valuables unattended. Many portables aren't connected to the school alarm system and are easy targets for break-ins.

Read your school, district, and benefits handbooks from cover to cover. If you haven't read them for a while, dust them off and read them again.

Be proud of your profession, your commitment, and your achievements. You worked hard to get where you are today. And yes, you *do* deserve your many holiday weeks!

Don't bring work home every night and every weekend. Take breaks to avoid burnout.

When was the last time you spent a day or weekend with your spouse or partner and didn't talk about work? Take out your calendar *now* and schedule some well-deserved time for the two of you.

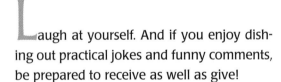

Laugh at yourself. And if you enjoy dishing out practical jokes and funny comments, be prepared to receive as well as give!

Keep a small personal care kit at your desk, complete with a toothbrush and toothpaste, deodorant, mouthwash, etc. If we want our students to sit near us after a lunchtime floor hockey game (or garlicky snack), let's make it a pleasant experience! And if a student ever offers you a breath mint . . . take it.

Once in a while, leave immediately after the school day ends. Relax and go for that hike or drive you've been promising yourself.

Keep an extra set of casual clothes and footwear at school. Then you'll be free to climb ropes in the gym, paint with your students, or trek through a marshy field to study plant life.

Find a quiet time during the school day when you can devote 5–10 minutes to yourself. Have a cup of tea, stretch, listen to music, close your eyes and breathe deeply, or read a few pages in a book. Recharge your batteries. Prep times and lunch breaks are good times to relax; if you have a free period, spend part of it doing something you enjoy.

Did you recently give a great lesson? Is a formerly bored or indifferent student inspired by an activity or assignment you created? Are students who once struggled to learn "getting it" when you teach them? Pause for a moment and savor your success.

Congratulate yourself for all of the wonderful things you do as a teacher. Reflect on times when you made your students laugh or gave a memorable lesson. Pat yourself on the back for times when you went out of your way to help a student study for a test, write a report, prepare for a speech, solve a problem, or grasp a concept. Reward yourself for a job well done.

Forgive yourself for making mistakes.

Building Relationships

Be friendly and courteous to the custodians, secretaries, and other support staff at your school — people whose jobs often go unnoticed. Learn their names and greet them when you see them; invite them to staff functions.

Let your students know that you respect your school's support staff and value the work they do. Have them write class thank-you notes. This teaches them to notice and appreciate others in their environment.

Invite aides, secretaries, custodians and other school workers to visit your classroom and talk about their jobs. Ask if they would like to demonstrate some of their work skills. Encourage questions and discussion.

Never make negative comments about other staff members in front of your students (or anyone else). If you have a problem with an individual, take it up with him or her in private. If that doesn't work, go through the appropriate channels, always communicating your willingness to arrive at a positive solution.

Compliment other staff members at every opportunity. This helps to develop a friendly and caring environment in your school and promotes self-esteem.

Do good deeds for other teachers, administrators, secretaries, custodians, school nurses, counselors, etc., "just because." They're all part of your school team, and it's important to keep spirits high. A thoughtful action, a smile, a joke, or a thank-you note can make someone's day.

Avoid giving office assistants rush jobs. Either plan ahead so they have enough time to prepare your memo or copy your test, or do it yourself. If you have access to a computer and your typing skills are reasonably good, there's no need to ask someone else to do your typing for you.

Eat lunch and take breaks with your peers regularly. Have a laugh, get to know each other better, share stories, and strengthen your sense of community.

There may be times when other staff members need to deal with your students in conflict or problem situations. Support their efforts and thank them for their help. Resist the urge to be overprotective or territorial.

Post a cartoon or joke in the mail room or staff room so your colleagues can start each morning with a smile.

Respect differences of opinion among your peers concerning educational issues, teaching strategies, etc. We're in the same profession, but we don't all share the same beliefs. Try not to take differences personally.

Don't talk about problem students, parents, or teachers in the staff lunchroom or lounge. Rumors can start, and it's unprofessional.

Take time during the day to visit with substitute teachers. Ask them how their day is going. Make them feel welcome; leave your name and room location in case they need to contact someone for help or support.

If a substitute teacher does a good job in your classroom, be sure to let your principal know. Thank the teacher and explain why you were happy with his or her work. Share the substitute's name with other staff members.

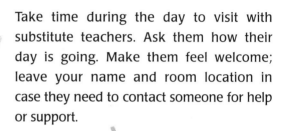

Organize a voluntary "secret pal" program for your school's staff. Those who choose to participate fill out a simple information sheet describing their favorite music, food, hobbies, etc., and anything else they want to tell about themselves, then drop their sheets into a box for a random drawing. Each participant draws one sheet to learn the identity of his or her "secret pal." For the rest of the term, semester, or year, make or do special things for your "pal" without revealing your identity. Once you commit to this activity, be sure to follow through!

Get together with teachers and administrators from other schools and talk about ways to share activities, supplies, resources, strategies, and functions. Do this weekly or monthly and build in some fun (playing floor hockey or softball, singing songs, sharing refreshments). Your students will benefit and you'll establish new friendships and connections.

Learn the names and telephone numbers of local newspaper reporters assigned to the education beat. Contact them personally and work to establish good relationships with them. Alert them to school and classroom events that are newsworthy and positive — student recognitions, awards, honor rolls, community action. Clear the details with your principal first.

Get to know the librarians in your school and public libraries. They can be valuable allies as you search for books, audiocassettes, multimedia materials, etc., to enhance your teaching. Honor their due dates and express appreciation for their help and expertise.

Find a mentor — someone you can call on to share ideas, discuss strategies, express problems and concerns, explore solutions, and brainstorm. Link up with a person who can give you advice, direction, and support when you need it.

Encourage your students to find mentors of their own — older students, other teachers, neighbors, or other adults in the community.

Drop in on other classrooms every once in a while (after clearing it with the teachers). Get to know the students. Praise the positive things you see — well-done projects, cooperation, effort. This strengthens the sense of community at your school and emphasizes that *all* teachers care about *all* students.

Practice tasteful practical jokes year round. This keeps your colleagues laughing and on their toes.

When one of your colleagues is having a hard time (professionally or personally), do what you can to help. Offer to mark tests, share supplies, or give up one of your own prep blocks to cover his or her class.

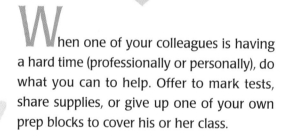

_S_hare new strategies and resources with your peers. _Example:_ When you return from workshops, conferences, and meetings, offer to share important items with interested staff members. If it's hard to get everyone together, jot down a few notes about what you have to offer, make copies, sign each copy, and drop them into staff members' boxes. Those who are interested will come to see you. If enough people want more information, schedule a mini-workshop. Sharing new strategies builds relationships and reinforces your own understanding of what you have learned.

When attending workshops, conferences, and meetings, carry several blank 3" x 5" cards (or a small notebook) in your purse or pocket. Jot down the names, phone numbers, and E-mail addresses of people who seem willing to share ideas or become pen pals with your class. Add a few words about them to jog your memory later. Contact them soon after you return to your classroom.

At workshops, conferences, and meetings, try to sit apart from your own staff members for at least part of each day. Give yourself a chance to meet educators from other schools and districts. You'll exchange strategies, share resources, and develop new friendships.

Never form opinions or make decisions based on rumor or hearsay. Give each individual the benefit of the doubt and get to know him or her on your own terms.

Do your best to get along with everyone on staff at your school, and treat all people with respect. Avoid cliques.

Follow your students' progress throughout the grades. This shows that you genuinely care about them as individuals. Take time to visit with former students who come to see you. When appropriate, invite them to address your new students.

If you need your principal's support for a special project or program, or if you just want some feedback on your teaching, invite him or her to visit your class. Extend your invitation in a note or in person, and be persistent; principals have busy schedules. Be prepared to have your principal walk in anytime.

When administrators visit your classroom, encourage them to participate as well as observe. See if they're willing to join a reading group, take part in a discussion, or get involved in a hands-on project. This will give them a real appreciation for what you do every day and how well you interact with your students.

Treat administrators as the valuable resources they are. Solicit their ideas, insights, and advice, and let them know that their opinions matter to you. The next time you want to try something a little bit offbeat or unconventional in your classroom, you're more likely to win their support.

As teachers, we love to be recognized for our expertise, and administrators are no different. Asking for help is a time-honored form of recognition.

Instead of waiting for administrators to reach out to you, why not reach out to them? Pick up the phone, send a note, make an appointment to stop by and say hello. They're people, too, and are probably more approachable than you think.

Many teachers feel intimidated by administrators, especially those at high levels (e.g., the superintendent). It helps to remember that most are former classroom teachers, so they know what it's like to be in your shoes.

From time to time, drop your superintendent a note about something positive that's happening in your classroom or school — improved attendance, rising test scores, students who are eager to learn, parent involvement, exciting projects. Keep administrators up-to-date on "good news" and they're more likely to help you when the news isn't so good.

Smiling is easy to do and it's free. If you present yourself as a happy, pleasant, cheerful person, you increase your chances of interacting with happy, pleasant, cheerful students and staff. A smile also shows that you're enjoying your job.

Becoming a Better Teacher

When you want to try new teaching strategies, techniques, or approaches, focus on one at a time. Stay with it until it feels comfortable before moving on to the next.

Check out your teaching wardrobe. Is it professional-looking and comfortable? Does it need updating?

On occasion, inject a little humor and/or color into your ensemble. Try a colorful jacket, a silly tie, patterned socks, or a bright scarf. Your students will be delighted.

Every once in a while, stop and ask yourself, "Am I doing all of the talking?" Few things are as tedious as a teacher who drones on and on.

Routines can get boring for everyone. If you always give the spelling test on Wednesday, move it to Friday. If each day begins with a science lesson, start with reading instead. Turn a whole day's schedule upside down — teach the last subject first and the first subject last.

Be flexible. Your way of teaching is not the only way, and it might not be the best way for some of your students.

Ask your principal to teach one of your lessons so you can observe your students in action. We miss a lot when we're teaching. Walk quietly around the room during the lesson; write down your observations and comments in a notebook; document trouble spots and areas of high attention and productivity. Review your notes later and make a list of things you'd like to change.

Find out what resources your school and/or district has to offer — audio-visual equipment, overhead projectors, computers, films, slides, maps, laser videodiscs, CD-ROMs, Internet connections, calculators, art supplies, prints, musical instruments, experts, consultants, etc. — and make full use of them.

Always have a Plan B. If a lesson isn't going well, switch to a backup lesson or activity.

How long has it been since you've reviewed your own grammar and spelling? Its not alright to make mistakes on the board and handouts; each error has it's tendency to multiply. (Can you find the three common errors in the preceding sentence?)

Monitor your speech habits. Do you overuse slang and fill your lessons with "ums," "likes," "ers," and "yeahs"? If you're not sure, ask a colleague to observe your teaching, or make a recording of yourself to review at home.

Several times during the school year, make an audio or video recording of your teaching. (Or have a student videotape you.) You'll learn a lot about your teaching.

Record yourself giving a lecture or a lesson, then listen to yourself critically and objectively. Could your speaking style use improvement? Do you talk too slowly or too quickly? Do you project your voice and avoid mumbling? Do you speak in a monotone? Try "peaks and valleys": Raise and lower your voice at appropriate points in sentences and paragraphs.

There will be times when you get angry — at individual students or groups, at your whole class, at interruptions, administrative decisions, red tape, whatever. View these as opportunities to model appropriate ways to deal with anger. Count to 10 (or 100), sit quietly, take your students on a brisk walk around the building, or do whatever works for you.

Learn about learning styles. Take a class, read a book, attend a conference, talk to your colleagues, or invite an expert in to speak. Adjust your teaching to your students' learning style preferences.

Welcome mistakes as excellent learning and teaching opportunities. Tell your students that you *expect* them to make mistakes. When you make a mistake, acknowledge it and take the proper steps — fix it if it's fixable, move on if it's not.

Many students feel intimidated by "perfect" teachers. Don't be afraid to let your weaknesses show. Demonstrate your willingness to take risks, knowing that you might make mistakes.

Work to narrow the gap between school and the "real world." Make lessons relevant to life outside the classroom; keep up with current events and discuss them with your students; have adult guest speakers describe how what they learned in school relates to their lives today.

If you don't know how to use a computer, learn as soon as you can. Start by finding out how much your students know about computers. You'll probably be amazed by the extent of their knowledge, and you may find your "teacher" among them.

If you don't know your way around the Internet, ask a student to show you how to "surf."

Never forget that you're shaping lives every day. What an awesome responsibility — and what a terrific opportunity — teaching is!

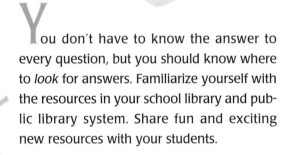

You don't have to know the answer to every question, but you should know where to *look* for answers. Familiarize yourself with the resources in your school library and public library system. Share fun and exciting new resources with your students.

Immediately after attending a workshop or conference, choose at least one new strategy you learned and incorporate it into your teaching. If you file the information for "later review," you might never use it. How many great ideas are gathering dust in forgotten files?

As teachers, we are role models whether we like it or not. Consider your appearance, gestures, language, attitude, etc. Remember that you have an impressionable audience.

Sometimes we teachers feel that we're supposed to know *everything.* If you're unsure how to complete a particular task, baffled by your new teacher's guide, or frustrated by a particular student (parent, colleague), get help.

Don't be afraid to say out loud, "I *love* learning and teaching."

Health
and Safety

Practice fire drills, earthquake drills, tornado drills, and emergency procedures each month or each quarter, and emphasize the importance of taking them seriously. Role play various situations. Practice controlled movement of your students under drill conditions.

Keep a fully-stocked first-aid kit in your classroom. Check it from time to time and replace any items that are old or depleted.

If you haven't been trained in CPR, the Heimlich Maneuver, and lab safety, sign up for training as soon as possible.

Come up with a procedure to follow when a student feels ill in school. The goals of any procedure should be to 1) immediately help the student, 2) cause the least amount of embarrassment to the student, and 3) cause the least amount of disruption to your class. Give permission for any student who suddenly gets ill to say "I'm sick; I have to leave" and exit the classroom for the restroom or the school nurse without further discussion. Hang a laminated hall pass on a hook by the door for emergencies.

Communicate with parents when a student gets sick in school; follow up with a phone call home. This shows that you are a caring teacher.

Learn about your students' physical needs as soon as possible. Read their files, talk to them and their parents, make observations, and set up simple exercises to help determine their strengths and weaknesses. Who has difficulty reading the board? Who has trouble hearing you? Do some students experience discomfort or pain during gym class? (Are these "growing pains," excuses for not wanting to participate, or physical conditions that need investigating?) Call on professionals – the school nurse, speech pathologist, social worker, hearing specialist, etc. – to help you assess your students' needs. Keep accurate and dated records throughout the year.

Try not to touch or rub your face during school hours unless you have washed your hands thoroughly. Doctors have found that teachers are especially prone to viruses. Wash your hands during breaks and enjoy a healthier, happier school year.

Ask your school nurse to check students for head lice as often as possible. (Have yourself checked, too.) Invite the nurse to your first open house or parent-teacher conferences to explain how to check for lice at home and what to do if they are found. Make it clear to students and parents alike that there is no connection between lice and economic or social status; lice don't discriminate!

Can your students move around the room without tripping over extension cords or wires? Do a thorough check to prevent accidents.

Make sure that students wear the necessary safety equipment when playing games and sports – helmets, masks, gloves, etc. If your school doesn't own the proper safety equipment for a particular game or sport, don't allow your students to play it.

Never ask or allow students to move televisions, stereos, heavy gym equipment, or other expensive and/or awkward equipment.

Pay attention to students' personal hygiene. Model and teach proper hygiene; involve school nurses and other professionals if necessary. If you notice a problem with a particular student, arrange to talk one-on-one with him or her. Be considerate and sensitive. If the problem persists, talk to the student's parents and/or your administrator.

Wander around the classroom and/or lunch-room when students are eating their lunches and snacks, and notice what they are eating. Poor nutrition can have a tremendous effect on student performance. Document your observations. Talk to your students about good nutrition; talk to parents during conferences and open houses. If you feel that certain students need special assistance, talk to your principal.

Read all labels on sprays, paints, chemical bottles, and all other arts, crafts, science, and cleaning supplies to make sure that proper safety precautions are taken. Review safety and first-aid procedures with your students prior to starting units and lessons where these supplies will be used.

It isn't uncommon for students to "feel sick" on test days or when big assignments are due. If you notice this happening regularly with some of your students, contact their parents. They may not be aware that their children are using "sickness" as an excuse.

When a student is absent due to illness for more than a day, call the parents. Express your concern and ask when the student will be returning to class. Arrange to have books and homework assignments sent home so the student won't fall behind.

Have plenty of tissues available in your classroom. Some teachers ask parents to help out by contributing a box of tissues at the start of the school year.

Keep a list of important "work numbers" — your principal, the substitute teachers' service — by your home phone in case of personal illness or emergency.

If you are ill, stay home. Your students will miss you, and you may be in the middle of an important series of lessons, but stay home anyway. Taking care of yourself benefits everyone.

General Tips for Effective Teaching

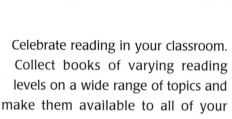

Celebrate reading in your classroom. Collect books of varying reading levels on a wide range of topics and make them available to all of your students. Encourage your students to bring their favorite books to class and share them.

Invite published authors to your school to teach classes, make presentations, or read from their writings.

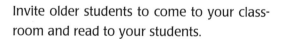

Invite older students to come to your classroom and read to your students.

Read aloud to your students, whether they're preschoolers or high school seniors. Being read to is a wonderful experience that shouldn't end at any age.

When you tell stories or read aloud, have your students sit close together in a group rather than at their desks. Even high school students will flop on the floor to hear a good story. Consider creating a reading corner with carpet scraps and oversized pillows.

Encourage your students to "live" the stories they read and hear in your classroom. Get them involved by using retelling and predicting strategies. Have them dramatize parts of the stories. Take stories into math, science, and gym lessons. Let your students experience what it would be like to be Aladdin, Hamlet, Anne of Green Gables, Tom Sawyer, Booker T. Washington, or Sojourner Truth.

Start book clubs in your classroom. Divide the class into small groups of 6–8 students. Every two weeks, set aside a half hour (or longer) for the groups to get together and discuss a story or book of their choosing. They can use the first meeting to brainstorm a list of things they might want to read over the next few months. Everyone should contribute at least two ideas. Each meeting ends with one student choosing the reading for the next meeting; the choice rotates around the group so everyone has a chance. Monitor the meetings but let the students run them. The point of this activity is to promote the fun of reading and encourage kids to talk about books and literature.

Before expecting students to read aloud to the class, give them ample practice time. You wouldn't want to give a command performance without the chance to prepare. Why should students be any different?

You can never have too many books in your classroom. Shop used book sales, library sales, garage sales, yard sales, etc., for books that might interest your students. Don't worry about age groups or reading levels; when students really want to know more about a subject, they won't mind tackling challenging material.

If you really want your students to love reading, don't assign written book reports.

Have students compile wish lists of books they'd like to have in the classroom. Ask parents to donate to your book fund.

Allow the free exchange of ideas and opinions in your classroom, but draw the line at back talk. Tasteful humor and joking at appropriate times are acceptable; rudeness and disrespectful language are not. Deal with any occurrences immediately and firmly.

Keep a Polaroid camera and film in your classroom at all times. You'll capture many special moments that may become excellent learning and teaching tools. The Polaroid company offers teacher workshops on how to use their cameras for teaching purposes. For more information, send an email to education@polaroid.com.

Use songs to teach messages and values. Go through a song one line at a time, sing it, and discuss the lyrics. A few titles to start with might include "Lean on Me," "We Are the World," and "What a Wonderful World." Invite students to bring in their own "message songs." Be sure to screen them before playing them for the class.

Your students will watch lots of television anyway, so give them some positive direction. Check the public TV listings at the start of each week, assign interesting programs for your students to watch, and discuss them in class.

Use problem solvers, brain teasers, puzzles, riddles, and jokes on a daily basis. They challenge minds, build skills, and spark creative discussions — and they're fun.

Have students design paper money in various denominations — $1, $5, $10 — and come up with a creative name (Dinodollars? Class Cash?). Make photocopies and establish a "bank." Assign dollar values to various behaviors — needing to borrow supplies, forgetting a signed permission slip, getting into trouble on the playground, not completing homework assignments — and give each student a set amount of "money" at the start of each week. Don't just "charge" students for problems; also "pay" them for good behavior, excellent work, cooperative group work, etc. Post the rules and values of the "money" where everyone can see them. Let students "cash in" at the end of each week for special activities or small treats available from the "class store."

When setting class goals and discussing ways to "earn" special rewards or activities, be realistic. Students will lose interest in a goal that takes several weeks or months to achieve. Shorter time frames are best for both elementary and secondary students.

Start a quotes collection. Watch for timely and inspiring quotations in magazines, newspapers, books, etc., that would be appropriate for your classroom. Print them out in interesting type fonts and display them around the room. Invite students to bring in their favorite quotes for display and discussion, or have them compile their own "quotes books" throughout the year.

Follow through with rewards and
consequences promptly and fairly.

Is the vocabulary you use in class appropriate for your students' age and ability? Don't bore them with vocabulary that's over their heads — or insult them with vocabulary that's beneath their capabilities. As you get to know your students, you'll learn how to enrich their vocabulary and challenge them without "losing" or frustrating them..

Give each student the opportunity to teach a mini-lesson. Ask for volunteers; this shouldn't be an assignment. Model the basic steps involved in teaching a lesson. Your students will gain appreciation for what you do and build teaching skills of their own. Even primary students are capable of teaching mini-lessons.

Support and enforce your school's dress code, if one exists. Talk privately with students who resist the dress code. Work together to come up with acceptable ways for them to express their individuality and personality. If you believe that the dress code is unreasonable, take it up with your administration.

Involve older students as positive role models in your school and put them in leadership positions. Let them earn special privileges during their last year of school. *Examples:* a dance at the end of every month, volleyball or floor hockey on Fridays, free periods.

If you teach in a religious school, then it's appropriate to discuss your religious beliefs in the classroom. If you teach in a public school, it's usually not appropriate. Your students probably come from a variety of faith traditions. Use your best judgment when determining when and whether to touch on different beliefs, and always keep such discussions within an educational context.

Tell your students how you expect them to behave in all kinds of situations — in the classroom, on field trips, on the playground, when there are visitors and substitutes, and so on. Be clear and explicit. Before students can meet (or exceed) our expectations, they need to know what they are.

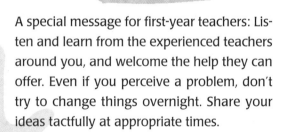

A special message for first-year teachers: Listen and learn from the experienced teachers around you, and welcome the help they can offer. Even if you perceive a problem, don't try to change things overnight. Share your ideas tactfully at appropriate times.

Another message for first-year teachers: Generally speaking, most of your colleagues will want to help you, and there will only be one or a few who may give you a hard time. Nobody has the right to boss you around, regardless of status or tenure. Communicate any ongoing problems to your principal.

Don't try to be best buddies with your students. Work with them, joke with them, get to know them, and enjoy their company, but avoid crossing the line to excessive familiarity. Some teachers learn this the hard way and end up battling to win their students' respect. Be fair, fun . . . and firm.

Preview all music videos and songs that students want to play in your classroom. Listen carefully to the lyrics. Many teachers have learned this lesson the hard way.

Preview all Internet Web sites before your students visit them. Check them out thoroughly — click on the links, read the messages, view the graphics, download the sound and video clips. Avoid surprises!

Monitor the environmental conditions in your classroom. Is the temperature constant and comfortable? Is the lighting adequate? Is there enough air circulation? If you feel that your students are struggling with sub-optimal conditions, talk to your principal.

From time to time, check out your classroom from your students' vantage points. Can everyone see the board, overhead projector screen, maps, etc.? Can everyone hear what you're saying when you're at the front of the room? What about students who sit next to the overhead projector, filmstrip projector, or VCR? Is the equipment noisy? Sit at several students' desks to see if there is a glare on the board or if equipment, furniture, or other students are obstructing their view.

When working with students at their desks or tables, make every effort to be at eye level with them. Short 7-year-olds would like to see something besides your nostrils, and tall 17-year-olds would like to see something besides your scalp!

Should students chew gum in class? Some teachers (and schools) say "no," but consider this: For students with attention problems or too much energy, chewing gum can help them to concentrate and stay on task. You might try making gum-chewing a privilege in your classroom. Students can chew if they agree to follow a few simple rules: 1) No loud chewing, smacking, or bubble-blowing; 2) No storing chewed gum under desks; 3) Dispose of gum properly (wrap it up and toss it in a wastebasket, not on the floor).

When you want your students to perform a task in a specific way, model it for them. This saves a lot of confusion. *Example:* If you expect the title page of a report to include the student's name at the upper right, the date at the lower right, and the title in the middle, draw an example on the board.

Before assigning seat work, go over the instructions and expectations with the class. Give students the chance to ask questions before they begin. Write any relevant page numbers and other important instructions or facts on the board so students can refer to them while they work.

Always remember that students are your top priority. It's easy to get so involved with conferences, committees, assemblies, extracurriculars, coaching, etc., that we forget this simple truth. Students come first.

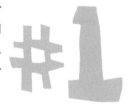

Allow plenty of practice time for students who will be giving speeches or presentations before a large group. If you let them practice on smaller audiences — two students, then four, then eight — this will help them build confidence before having to face the whole class or school.

Help students prepare for classroom performances, presentations, and speeches by showing a brief video on a related topic. Every 10–15 seconds, turn off the sound or darken the picture. When the sound is off, instruct students to focus on the person's facial expressions, gestures, and body position; when the picture is off, have them concentrate on the voice, tone, and emphasis. Resume regular play following each interlude. Afterward, discuss with the students what they saw and heard, then show the video again in its entirety.

Instead of trying to give instructions while students are lining up, collecting materials, or moving around the room, wait for silence.

Model appropriate and acceptable behaviors for your students. Use role plays, question-and-answer sessions, and visits from the school counselor. Teach students to recognize potential problems before they erupt; teach them to make good choices about their own behavior. Prevention is the best cure.

Student journals should be places for free-flowing, unselfconscious writing. Never correct grammar, spelling, and punctuation in a journal. If you want to communicate with your students through their journals — responding to thoughts and ideas, asking questions, adding words of encouragement — do it in pencil or blue pen, never red pen. (Positive comments only!)

Before beginning a new unit of study, ask your students what they know about the topic. (They may already know much of what you are planning to teach.) Based on what you learn from them, you may be able to skip ahead to a better starting point. If you find that the unit is too advanced for most of your students, 1) back up and prepare them for what they will be learning, 2) reschedule the unit for later in the year, or 3) let those students who are ready pursue the unit as an independent study or project.

Don't assume that your gifted students are gifted in every area. Similarly, don't assume that your students with LD are learning disabled in every area. (Instead of "learning disabilities," consider using the term "learning differences," since there's less negativity attached to it.)

Be careful not to single out your gifted students for special treatment or privileges. Students of all ages are quick to notice favoritism, which usually breeds resentment.

Give students who have difficulty learning in traditional ways (reading, writing, listening) plenty of opportunities to learn in other ways: with manipulatives, multimedia materials, computers, etc.

Avoid stereotyping students, teachers, or parents based on their appearance, family background, income level, ethnic origins, etc. Treat everyone as an individual who is worthy of respect.

Look through your textbooks, workbooks, posters, and other classroom materials for signs of cultural bias, stereotyping, racism, and sexism. Which materials need updating or replacing?

Share and exchange ideas with your peers, but don't try to copy their teaching styles. Be yourself.

If other teachers make negative comments about activities your students enjoy doing, thank them for their input and continue with the activities.

When you accept poor-quality work from your students, you're not helping them. Instead, you're sending the message that you think they're not capable of high-quality work.

Resist the temptation to "rescue" students who are having trouble learning. This creates dependency and promotes helplessness.

Never give up on any student. We all experience frustration at times, and we all have days when we wish that certain students were someone else's problem. Focus on small goals and gains and find humor wherever you can. Remember that you're not alone in your profession. Ask for help when you need it.

Communicating
with Parents

Early in the school year, send home a note inviting parents to communicate with you regularly and often. Include your telephone number at school and the hours when you're available to take calls. Encourage parents to drop you a note whenever they have a question or concern, and ask them to be sure to include their name, the date, their daytime and evening telephone numbers, and their signature on any correspondence they send to you.

Sometime during the first week of school, send home a brief parent survey. Invite parents to tell you about their jobs, talents, hobbies, and areas of expertise. Ask if they'd be willing to talk to your class. As you read through the completed surveys, match parents to upcoming units and topics. Have parents come to class as guest speakers throughout the year.

Very early in the school year, send a letter to parents explaining your homework policies and expectations. Stay within school and/or district guidelines for your grade level. Explain that even on days when homework isn't assigned, students should spend their homework time working on something that will improve their learning skills. *Examples:* reading a book, looking at a newspaper, practicing math problems, watching an educational program on television.

As often as you can throughout the year, send notes to parents commenting on something positive you have observed about their children.

Keep parents informed about events in your classroom. Consider compiling a weekly or monthly newsletter for students to bring home. Report on exciting lessons and projects; "feature" individual students; have students contribute brief articles about favorite activities.

If you must report "bad news" — a behavior problem, incomplete homework, a poor grade or test performance — always do it in private (by phone, face-to-face conference, or personal note) and preface it with a positive comment.

Be aware of students whose parents are divorced and share custody. Students who live in more than one home may show patterns of absenteeism. Investigate when necessary, and work with the parents and students to arrive at a solution.

Keep a log of phone conversations with parents. For each conversation, note 1) the parent's first and last names, 2) the student's name, 3) the time and date of the call, 4) who initiated the call, and 5) the reason for the call. Jot down any comments and action items. Consult your log at report card time and throughout the year; you'll find that it's a valuable source of information and documentation.

Keep a file of notes you receive from parents — explanations of student absences, requests for excused absences, etc. Review your files from time to time and look for patterns. Do some students regularly "get sick" before certain classes, tests, activities, or events? If so, talk to the students one-on-one and try to resolve the problem. Contact the parents, explain the situation, and ask for their support.

The week before parent-teacher conferences are scheduled to begin, send notes home reminding parents of the date, time, and duration of their conferences. Include a brief agenda so parents know what to expect. The bottom half of the agenda might be a "cut-out-and-return" form where parents can write any questions and/or concerns they would like to address during the conference. This gives everyone a chance to think about the conference in advance and ensures that the time allowed is used efficiently and productively.

When possible, invite students to attend conferences with their parents. You'll be talking about them and their performance, so why not include them?

Have students lead at least one parent-teacher conference during the year. Put them in charge of the agenda, format, refreshments, and demonstrations (of portfolios, work samples, etc.). Allow time for rehearsals before the actual event.

Instead of asking students to relay messages to their parents, communicate with parents directly in writing or by telephone. When requesting a written response, include a self-addressed envelope.

When planning "messy" activities (art projects, outdoor projects), send a note home to parents several days in advance explaining what their children will be doing, how they should dress, and what (if anything) they should bring to safeguard against stains and spills.

Encourage parents to help in the classroom. Offer mini-workshops for parent volunteers to review procedures and guidelines and answer questions. Willing, committed, energetic parents can do a lot to enhance the learning environment.

Monitor your parent helpers. If they have difficulties, it's your job to help them. Encourage them to come to you with questions, concerns, and observations.

Thank your parent helpers often. Invite them to class functions and make them feel welcome. Have students create thank-you cards. Work with the other teachers and staff to hold a "Parent Appreciation Night" at the end of the school year.

Homework
and Tests

Have students keep track of their homework assignments in a "homework book" (small spiral-bound notebook or datebook) that goes home daily. Teach them how to organize and prioritize their assignments. Students who have difficulty remembering or completing assignments should have a parent sign their homework book each night. Explain that when they're back on track, the signatures won't be necessary.

Make sure that homework assignments are absolutely clear. List them on the board with a due date beside each one. Also list any textbooks, notebooks, worksheets, and other materials needed to complete the homework. Explain what you expect students to do for each assignment and when and where you want them to hand in their finished work. Establish firm but reasonable consequences for late assignments.

Don't expect parents to be educators. It's not their job to teach their children how to compose an essay, memorize multiplication tables, or master a new skill. The homework you assign should reinforce what your students are learning in your classroom; it shouldn't require new learning. If students have difficulty completing their homework, spend class time teaching the skills and concepts they need.

Follow up on incomplete homework assignments. Do your students have valid excuses for not doing their homework? If not, why not? Communicate with parents so assignments don't fall between the cracks and students don't fall too far behind.

Homework shouldn't be "busy work." Instead, it should reinforce what students are learning, provide needed practice, and strengthen skills. Students who have clearly mastered a particular concept or skill shouldn't have to do homework that is boring and repetitive for them. Those who haven't yet grasped a concept or skill shouldn't be given homework that is beyond their capabilities.

Mark and return assignments and tests as soon as you possibly can. The longer the waiting period, the weaker the teachable moment. A quick response shows your students that their work is a priority.

Correct tests and assignments in short work periods with frequent breaks in between. Accuracy suffers when you're tired or your mind wanders.

When marking student work, try not to get caught in the neatness trap. Sometimes teachers place students in different "camps" based on handwriting, presentation, and other characteristics that are essentially cosmetic. Recognize neatness, but never at the expense of content or quality.

Communicate with other teachers about homework policies and expectations. Are they consistent from class to class? Try to stagger homework assignments and long-term projects so students aren't overloaded at various points during the year.

Work that isn't done properly should be redone on the students' own time. Most students will learn quickly that it's better to do something right the first time than to spend part of a lunch break or recess doing it over.

Clip corners of completed and corrected pages in student notebooks. This makes it easy to turn to the most recent page or the next new page without flipping through. Share this simple strategy with your students; they might want to try it in their assignment notebooks or daily calendars.

When preparing tests, don't include questions on topics that haven't been covered in the classroom. Unless you're giving a pretest, there's no point in testing students on material they don't know.

During test times, space your students around the room so wandering eyes don't get a workout. Observe your students during the test and make notes on behaviors you may want to discuss with them later. *Examples:* looking at the clock every few minutes, nervous tapping, etc. Do some students "choke" during test conditions? Do others fly through tests without checking their answers?

Record the time when each student hands in his or her test. This information can help you to identify students who need to slow down (or speed up).

Begin each written test by going over the instructions with your students and answering any questions they might have about how to proceed.

Have students initial each page of a test to indicate that they have checked their answers. Don't accept a test that hasn't been initialed.

Create a quiet and comfortable environment for your students during tests. Hang a "Do Not Disturb" sign on your door. Provide scratch paper and extra pens, pencils, and erasers. Make sure that the room is well ventilated and properly lit.

Try to allow for individual learning styles during tests. If one student prefers to sit on the floor, another wants to face the wall, and another needs to take frequent stretch breaks, these actions shouldn't cause problems as long as they don't disturb the other students.

Don't grade on the curve. Give students the grades they really earn. If all of your students earn A's or B's on the history test, then those are the grades you should give them. (Of course, you might want to make the next test harder!)

Beyond Your Classroom

On occasion, wander through your school and take a look around. Observe hallways, common areas, and other classrooms. Take notes, recording positive comments and concerns. Share your observations with your principal.

Learn the names of as many students as you can, not just those in your own classroom. Greet them by name when you see them in the halls, cafeteria, library, etc.

Has your administration ever surveyed the staff about their interests, passions, talents, hobbies, collections, and special abilities? If not, suggest that a survey be done. Offer to help prepare and distribute it. You'll be amazed at what you learn about your colleagues.

Once you have the results of a staff survey, use them. Invite teachers to share their interests, talents, etc., with your class. Create a special bulletin board — perhaps titled "Things You Didn't Know About Your Teachers!" — with photographs and brief descriptions. *Examples:* "Mr. Miller, Monster Truck Driver!" "Ms. DeMarco, Photographer!" "Mr. Muñez, Gourmet Chef!" "Mrs. Li, Champion Poodle Trainer!"

Before taking a field trip, make a trial run. Visit the location; check out the facilities; find out who will be there on the day you visit with your class; preview films, videos, presentations, and exhibits. Call ahead on the day before your field trip to confirm that you're expected.

If your school has a P.A. system, start a radio-style program that includes daily announcements, game scores, news items, birthdays, upcoming events, etc. Some schools hold contests such as "Name That Tune," "Mystery Person," and "What Am I?" Students pick up an answer form, fill in the answers to clues that are given during the announcements, then hand in the forms to teachers (or drop them in an answer box). The answers and winners' names are shared during the next radio spot. You might give your program a catchy title, use music, and train students to be D.J.s.

Have your gym routine down to a fine art. Make sure that everyone knows proper changing procedures (if your students change clothes for gym), warm-up activities, cool-down activities, and where to line up when they're ready to return to class. Write 4–5 warm-up activities on the gymnasium board for students to start with as soon as they enter the gym. It's a waste of time to make everyone wait until the whole group is ready.

When addressing assemblies, model good public speaking skills. Warm up your voice ahead of time; speak clearly and with confidence; vary your tone as you speak; add gestures to words; make eye contact with audience members.

Model community service and volunteerism for your students. Get involved and keep your students informed of what you do. If you help to feed homeless people or volunteer at a nursing home, perhaps some of your students will want to join you.

Encourage your students to serve others. Do your local retirement homes, hospitals, heritage societies, recycling groups, plant-a-tree projects, etc., need help? Research several possibilities and have the class vote on one that interests them. Draft a letter with your students to the organization and explain that you would like to get involved. Invite parents to participate. Clear all projects with your principal before proceeding.

If you ever see students or staff being verbally, physically, or sexually abused, report it *immediately* to the appropriate authorities, following guidelines set forth in your school or district handbook. In many cases, this is the law; in all others, it's common sense.

When you are on supervision duty, keep moving. Constantly look around, make observations, and cover both inside and outside areas. Greet individual staff members and students, be friendly, but don't engage in lengthy conversations that may hold you to one spot. Bring along a notepad and pencil for taking notes.

Gain a better understanding of your school's curriculum by talking to the teachers of the grades before and after yours. Communicate expectations, share problems and solutions, and plan together to avoid duplicating units and lessons — especially important if you teach more than one grade or age group.

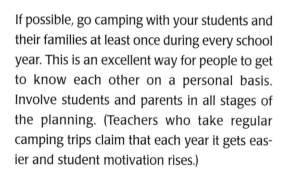

If possible, go camping with your students and their families at least once during every school year. This is an excellent way for people to get to know each other on a personal basis. Involve students and parents in all stages of the planning. (Teachers who take regular camping trips claim that each year it gets easier and student motivation rises.)

Teach your students about money and money management. Bring in catalogs, flyers, and price lists; have students go "shopping" on a budget. Some teachers take their students on "shopping trips" to local malls — complete with calculators and parent helpers — so students can price out lists of items they want to "buy."

Attend school functions in which your students are participating — plays, choir concerts, band concerts, athletic events, dance recitals, debate competitions, spelling bees, etc. — and root for them.

Once a week or at least once a month, have lunch with your students in the school cafeteria. Lunchtime conversations can be very entertaining (and revealing). Give the cafeteria food a try. If you agree that it's really as bad as your students say it is, tell the principal.

Celebrations
and
Special Events

Keep a "Celebrations Box" in your classroom. Invite students to suggest fun activities for everyone to do. (Preview them before adding them to the box so "take a class trip to Disney World" doesn't end up as one of the choices.) When the class achieves a predetermined goal, draw a suggestion from the "Celebrations Box" and enjoy.

Arrange or participate in activities throughout the school year that involve both students and teachers. Sports, lunchtime games, sing-alongs, art projects, school clean-ups, community service projects, plays, etc., are just a few examples of activities that can bring students and teachers together as a team.

Every so often, surprise your students with spontaneity. Stop a lesson and play a game, sing a few songs, have a silly stretch, tell jokes, or take a walk.

Recognize students' birthdays as special events. Develop classroom rituals — sing-alongs, cards made by students, birthday balloons filled with jellybeans, special privileges for the day, etc. Display a birthday calendar for students to monitor; let those whose birthdays fall on holidays or during breaks choose "alternate birthdays" to celebrate with the class. Remember that not all religious faiths celebrate birthdays, and give students the option of not participating.

Schedule school-wide events around fun and sometimes silly themes: "Dress-Up Day," "Cartoon Day," "Ice-Cream Day," "Inside-Out Day" (when everyone wears their clothes inside-out). Students and staff can work together to plan special activities. Festive events like these can bring your whole school together, improving relationships, communication, school spirit, and the learning environment.

*S*chedule "Student Recognition Days" to honor students who excel in areas other than athletics and academics. Invite teachers to nominate students who volunteer to help with school or classroom tasks, exhibit a positive attitude, enhance the classroom environment, or simply brighten their day. Plan after-school or evening recognition ceremonies and invite parents to attend. Present the students with special certificates and publicize their contributions in the daily announcements, school newspaper, and local newspapers.

Hold at least five parties a year in your classroom — to celebrate holidays, the end of a term, the coming of a new season, a successful performance, etc. Get students involved in planning these special events. Celebrate your accomplishments as a team and have fun! Remember to consider students who have food allergies, those who are diabetic, and those who are not allowed to participate in certain kinds of parties due to their religious beliefs.

Schedule annual or semi-annual student appreciation events and invite family members. Share student work, put on brief performances, and involve family members in activities. These gatherings should be informal and enjoyable celebrations of learning (stories, project work, murals, computer skills, basketball skills, etc.), not displays of "perfect" work. Every student should be represented.

Once every quarter (or more often), set aside your lesson plans for a class period or an afternoon and announce a "mini-vacation." Students can work on art projects, play games, read, watch videos, listen to audiocassettes, or anything they choose, provided they keep the noise level down to a low roar and treat each other respectfully. Go from student to student or group to group to see what they're doing, ask and answer questions, and share in the fun.

Broaden the science fair concept to encompass other subject areas. What about an inventors' fair? A writers' fair? A music fair? A sports fair?

Have your students create class yearbooks as keepsakes at the end of the year. Photocopy student and class pictures taken during the year; include student stories and a calendar of the year's events; leave room for students to add their own comments. Students can exchange and sign their yearbooks on the last day of school.

Wear a clown nose, rabbit ears, fuzzy bedroom slippers, funny hat, or zebra-print suspenders to class one day. Act like your usual self and see what happens.

About the Authors

Craig Mitchell has taught elementary school in British Columbia for sixteen years. He has a Bachelor of General Studies (B.G.S.) and a Graduate Diploma in Literacy from Simon Fraser University. He has taught seven different grade levels and has experience as a head teacher and support teacher. Craig worked as a Faculty Associate at Simon Fraser University where he helped student teachers develop their teaching skills. He is presently teaching at the third grade level in an elementary school which operates on a modified calendar. Craig resides with his wife, Melanie, and their two daughters, Bethany and Tiana, in Maple Ridge, B.C.

Pamela Espeland has written or coauthored several books for children and adults including *Life Lists for Teens, What Kids Need to Succeed, What Teens Need to Succeed, Making the Most of Today, Making Every Day Count, Stick Up for Yourself!,* and *Bringing Out the Best.* She received her B.A. from Carleton College in Northfield, Minnesota.

Other Great Books from Free Spirit

Jump Starters
Quick Classroom Activities That Develop Self-Esteem, Creativity, and Cooperation
by Linda Nason McElherne, M.A.
Features fifty-two themes within five topics: Knowing Myself, Getting to Know Others, Succeeding in School, Life Skills, and Just for Fun. For teachers, grades 3–6.
$21.95; 184 pp.; softcover; illus.; 8½" x 11"

Laughing Lessons
149⅔ Ways to Make Teaching and Learning Fun
by Ron Burgess
What's one of the best ways to get through to kids in your classroom? Lighten up! Even if you think you might be "humor impaired," this book can help you make your classroom a fun and lively place. If you take your job very seriously, this book is for you. For teachers, grades K–5.
$21.95; 208 pp.; softcover; illus.; 8" x 10"

To place an order or to request a free catalog of
SELF-HELP FOR KIDS® *and* SELF-HELP FOR TEENS® *materials,*
please write, call, email, or visit our Web site:

Free Spirit Publishing Inc.
217 Fifth Avenue North • Suite 200 Minneapolis, MN 55401-1299
toll-free 800.735.7323 • local 612.338.2068 • fax 612.337.5050
help4kids@freespirit.com • www.freespirit.com